Eiko & Koma

NEW DIRECTIONS POETRY PAMPHLETS

Eiko & Koma

Forrest Gander

Photographs by Anna Lee Campbell

NEW DIRECTIONS POETRY PAMPHLET #8

ACKNOWLEDGMENTS
LyrikLine, Spring 2011, Claudia Keelan, ed: "Faithfulness," "Rust," "Entanglement"
Eiko & Koma: Retrospective Catalogue, Walker Art Center, 2011, Joan Rothfuss, ed: "Schematic"
Paris Review, Fall 2011, Robyn Creswell, ed: "Then he deflowers her ..." as "Body Visible"
The Baffler, Spring 2012, Albert Mobilio, ed: "Projecting Love"
Lana Turner: a Journal of Arts & Criticism, Calvin Bedient, ed., Fall 2013: "Mourning," "The Caravan Project," "Caravan Garden," "When Nights were Dark," "River," "Raven," and "Buried."

Cover design by Office of Paul Sahre
Interior design by Eileen Baumgartner and Erik Rieselbach
Manufactured in the United States of America
New Directions Books are printed on acid-free paper.
First published as New Directions Poetry Pamphlet #8 in 2013
Published simultaneously in Canada by Penguin Books Canada Limited

Library of Congress Cataloging-in-Publication Data
Gander, Forrest, 1956–
[Poems. Selections]
Eiko & Koma / Forrest Gander.
pages ; cm. — (A New Directions poetry pamphlet; #8)
ISBN 978-0-8112-2094-1 (alk. paper: acid-free paper)
I. Title. II. Title: Eiko and Koma.
PS3557.A47E37 2013
811'.54—dc23

2013005430

10 9 8 7 6 5 4 3 2 1

New Directions Books are published for James Laughlin
by New Directions Publishing Corporation
80 Eighth Avenue, New York 10011

CONTENTS

"All spirit in the end becomes bodily visible."
—*Friedrich Nietszche*

"The spirit has no voice, because where there is voice there is body."
—*Leonardo Da Vinci*

"The soul and the body have an extreme conjunction."
—*Michel de Montaigne (in his copy of Lucretius)*

FAITHFULNESS

A life might change a
person's life might change with
a gesture or shaping
phrase in albumen flare
and gentleness from which
gestate bodies
wake supple
odd as an oyster

her nostrils' dilation slow
contraction of his ribs breeze
in the mulch (lifebreath)
as she clutches
herself his thumb
palpates
her jaw and neck

marmoreal contour the long
curving spine-trough
each lumbar vertebrae (one by
one) distinguishable
undulations blade-
out from his shoulders
her everted heel
drawn up by ligaments
in her calf so

between them
space (a uni-
verse in zygote) might

be reconceived as a
  means of access flesh realm
    blind finding flesh blindly
      feeling forward the apical arm
        spasms in prelight
          feet flat under
            her hips palms
              down the whole frame
                lifting ventral upward and

                  buckling as though
                    newborn or unused
                      to this weight or sequence
                  a tendon behind
                the synovial bursa
              (exquisitely) testing its range
            legfolded under
          her body swaying
        rises again spavined
          thighs elbows incurved
            against the joint

                  probing air
                    with his face
                    his lissome trunk dragged
                    forward on (armpinned)
                  shoulder stumps
                broken momentums
            thigh waves
            from pelvic socket

            as they fall awkward
          to proscenium

clavicle pockets of shadow
(openmouthed) foot-cocked
their heads arched back
on throats rhymed
mouth and eyes capsized
and four buttocks a
madrigal pear shifting
equilibrium of force
as he disencoils her
waist a fountain her
nape goes slack and hair sweeps
the floor such
solemnity in becoming
aware of
emotion while

silence chews edges
of water-sound   night   wind
his hands
ardent vulnerable
great toe withdrawn
from the immensity
of contact clockwork
articulate (fanfingered)
imploring
first figures
spent and mutual with a world
two bodies
releasing the event

SCHEMATIC

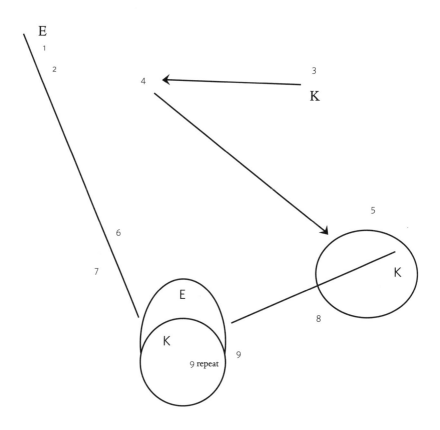

[1] forestalling step, irrational lift of wrist

[2] breathing through skin, blow arms out

[3] arrow stage right, sucking air

[4] lingering six heartbeats, splay thumbs, resisting inertia

[5] monkey-pant Ai! (愛), contract right buttock, going yellow

[6] reversing shoulder forward, cleaving, limpfalling away

[7] Koma mirroring, Eiko mirroring

[8] release weight upward, offering throat, constellate center stage

[9] orthogonal eyebeams, stopping breath, radiate stillness

★　　　★　　　★

Then he deflowers her, pulling away the greenery.
Then a blue vein thinning into a hollow.
Then it is the hollow between her neck and lower jaw.
Then spaced ligaments twitching in his forearm.
Then connected in lightlessness they are.
Then by an invisible capillary network.
Then balancing on her nates, her legs in the air waving.
Then he returns with a limp.
Then into her bent spine.
Then she is grabbing at unused air over her head.
Then is he inching edgewise turning his face.
Then offers her his armload of giftstraw and loose ash.
Then staggering away horrified.
Then coming toward him, hands upward, palms out.

RUST

What are they? Orchids.
Bluelit against the chainlink fence.
Four legs tendriling.

What are they? Captured
by the spot. Chins
tucked to their chests.

What are they? Incarcerated orchids.
Her legs tipping, in slow pulses,
toward him. He rolls

to his scapula. What
are they? Jail break. His weight
on his neck and shoulders.

A leg, one of her inverted legs
brushes his inverted torso. Body
curling around his body. In pulses,

lento, lento, she crosses over
him. What are they? She goes
placid and supine and then her legs

climb the fence and
his and darkness.

MOURNING

                    activates her
            crooked knee as
                          a frame for
his face
          for his
                  intimacy for
his violence
         against her

PROJECTING LOVE

dragging her fingernails across the air as

stage left, he steps from darkness into his flesh

under the minatory glare the flexed

tendons of his fingers, her eyes and

lips flare when he stumbles

she is aware without looking

almost they embrace

vessels and nerves of his cheek under

a thin strata of fascia when

her mouth breaks black open

when stage right he exits cupping the wound

when she cries out (in Japanese)

"I see the world upside down"

THE CARAVAN PROJECT

Within the trailered cave, they are poulticed by moss, their whitened bodies lifting, pokily, like trilliums from a bryophitic carpet. Elbow leading, her arm upheaves the hanging moss and lets it fall. Abstractedly, he plucks a stick dangling from the roofmass. At certain angles, the gauze over their faces opaques and renders them featureless. We stand waiting.

And they too, seem to be waiting. Even on their hours-long torturous dawdling peregrinations, they seem to be waiting. As though each expected the other to disclose a purpose, their mutual purpose. As if the moss might offer its revelation. As if their faces were ever to be the embryos of some gestating surprise. Or it is as though he has forgotten all about her and she has forgotten him and then they happen to glimpse each other and so sedately raise their hands in unison, in semi-recognition, quivering, the web across his face and arm quivering as with the memory of sentiment, a memory gauzy and webbed as they themselves are webbed with sleep and underworld, and how long can such imminence be sustained? They are two question marks in a terrarium and she has crawled now onto the ledge and paused, and he is springing up now on his toes as if to ascend, as if to initiate the decisive act, with every tension clapping to the arches of his feet, to his bulbous calves, their striated thew, and then he cannot remember what that act might be, the toes speculatively gripping and releasing before the heels lower themselves and touch ground again and the soles reconsider their accustomed load. And she has already turned, in any case, inside herself, unroused.

BREATH

Early draft of the world. Or

has all that came before
made them
its repository? Grove of slash.
They are. Flowerless dirt.

Windmoan over
leafy mound strewn
with two human forms,
veined and branched. To

become what one was: that
never happens. But now the
ground wrinkles with
their languorous

pandiculation. Crescent
shoulder blade and blue
bays between expanding,
contracting ribs. That the

recognizable mammalian
familiarity recedes in
exposures, in dilated time.
Become one, inhuman, beyond

animal. Are they.

CARAVAN GARDEN

Abandoned egg yawing, behind, drooplets, uterine crown fire,
their, torsos sway, heads wag silently, bestir themselves,
keening from, half mineral half, leaf, a palisade of scarlety, bristles,
gauze globule, delicate-like, chrysalid, bestirred separately, upward,
twisting
into space, antennary plumes, dangle, red-lit, gnawed,
his wrists, bounded by arteries, their torsos, pendulate, from igne-
ous moss,
rich in pith, and retted, into limpness with their, sweat, bridal night,
degorged here, the force
that drives her forward, of counter-desire, absolute,
physical apprehension, they will choose, are choosing have, chosen,
to participate, like adjacent colors,
skin, talc, cracked stalks, pausing, filling with, eye-lorn,
lavender and citronella nest,
delicately, caught in

PARABLE

Cool halogen beam on
      pelt-covered
            human limbs

Lamp dims

Man stumbles from
      burnt curtain
            toward recumbent what?

Placing a white
      bowl with kill
            holes over her face

No

Placing a wreath
      of raven feathers
            over her face

Shaking his head
      his spreading
            teeth ventilate

The black
      spindle-whorl
            in his mouth

She coughs up
    breath she
        suffocating rises

She rises to her knees
    he forces her down
        with his foot
            she rises he
                plants his heel
            in her scapula and
        flattens her

Face-smack

Floods up full

Taken by surprise he is
        limping away
            stage right on

His good foot
    staring behind him
        terrified and heavenward

WHEN NIGHTS WERE DARK

                    enthroned
        pressed   together
        in the   (they)   wombish
    wet glow in   (are in)   cerise semi-
eclipse overhung   (place and)   with spume
stripped   (it is)   they are
cocooned but   (of them)   seen as through
    a rip   an imploring
                    open mouth

CONVERGENCE

so sever   their link
with the sure
      and disturb
the river's   equilibrium
going still   stilling as
cold   flesh tingles
in water   and

to refuse withdrawal   his gape
and arms trailing   snapped
branches   immersed
      in an excursion
that the soul   might be called
into   her face

double specter   afloat
in nightfluid   honeys and
reds of skin-   glow
and at their   common
brink   her jaw offers
its underthroat   he hauls her
in   their eyes won't
touch her   fingers

unresponsive   limply
bundled   in his grasp
      fugitive counter-
part   late-day shoals
against her arm   when he
releases her   into the drift
and she   startles

RIVER

Taut current, throughstricken
with night, starbit,

and both of them
facing off. En-
igma tipped to
distortion—*

She floats on swirled
obsidian current. Their
sightlines swim across
each other. Stars
don't look away
from the unfolding,

the going alluvial,
she against his
tenderness.

*cutaway:
        to the blanks in her face-slots

RAVEN

Until they sound each other   they scrape
around in confines of blindness   skin

on skin as mind   peering overhead

at her own hand   exposed
ardency   foot fully-pointed

The carotid takes its (slightly)   curved
course north of his breastbone

then it finishes   (his white flower breath)
and the head loosens from   its stem

falling back unsupported

He accepts the straw   as her gift
sacrum to   sacrum his fingers

at her ear her   hair swallows his wrist
Of some mutilated offering   these are the

black feathers   the canoe-bone in her shin
and ashes from his body rising

ENTANGLEMENT

And begin to emerge. From their
long float. From cellars of sleep.
Here on the earth's wet
set. Hair and leaves mixed
with leaves and hair. Vision sheared
to make room for vision.
Two figures and
the caesura of
longing. Bound by what is
unwritten. Unwakened,

their eyes done in.
Slack-mouthed and presymbolic.
Her great toe stiffens
with vegetal slowness. Their heads
roll up, throat offered each
to each. Elocutionary
earthsheen. The fibrous muscles
in his thighs twitching. As god

pours into the creatural. Still,
receptive
to and flush
with ground's swell. They
do not move in the same world
in which we observe them.

Upright, they are at risk. Her
neck pulling birdlong against
her shoulder. He wobbles, spasmodic,
toward her, through invisible web.
Her in-bent arms spread
like a cormorant's. Emphatically
angular. His hand, his hand
feeling for her face. This
as love story.

This as love story. His hand,
his hand feeling for her.
Face, emphatically angular. Her in-bent
arms spread like a cormorant's.
He wobbles toward her, spasmodic,
through invisible web. Her
neck pulling birdlong against.
Her shoulder, upright. They
are. At risk, they do not

move in the same world
in which we observe them.
Receptive to and flush
with ground's swell, still.
As the creatural pours
into god. The

fibrous muscles in his thighs
twitching. Earthsheen.
Elocutionary, their
heads roll up, throat offered
each to each. Her great
toe stiffens with vegetal
slowness. Presymbolic,
slack-mouthed, unwakened.

Their eyes done in, bound
by. What is unwritten? Two figures.
And the caesura of longing.
Vision shears away
to make room for vision. Leaves
and hair mixed with hair
and leaves. Here
on the earth's wet set. From
cellars of sleep, from their
long float. And begin
to emerge.

STAGE LEFT

Deformed into reverie, the vision
survives our initial fascination

and fills with demi-sleep. As air moves
for what strops it. As space is made

incomplete by gesture.

Slaughtered arc-flicker
splashes onto them.

Their world without odors. Our
gawking in shared solitude. She adopts

positions antecedent to
verticality. Falling,

he is always inside
himself falling.

In their moment of transfiguration,
our fleshly paroxysm of feeling.

Twined in a feral *pas de deux*.
Probing

the whole register
in riveting shifts of fissiparity and durance

that mete our breath.

BURIED

Unpacks the recognizable its chaos here
        and the composition stutters Face
                stalking itself from inside beyond

all levels of—Compressed into looking
        unplotted brutal adust His back
                muscles Her ribcage splays They are naked

filled with the enormity of naked
        stillness Head held up Her hair
                pierced Quills fixed to her back

and her right knee bent to her face
        The air muffled through which his looking
                flies from somnolent eyes beyond

walls that mark another beyond
        of rooms echoey with shoe-scuffs naked
                squeaks Fully stretched he looks

up Bows his neck His hair
        pouring to the floor as his face
                lifts chin tilting back-

wards toward the audience seated back
        from the stage on benches in a beyond
                of dim-out from which they face

the mound of ordure with naked
        bodies on either side Blue-black hair
                soft as a negative of two matchflames Look

at the splice of likeness then look
        again It is severed They turn their backs
            as waterdrops pop here

and here across the dirt and beyond
        in dim penetralia Naked
                sound of waterdrops in the quiet Her face

fissures Her mouth a rictus Her face
        in its final expression An unsustainable look
                into another dimension Of what? His naked

hand a piece of music boosted into the black
        as we in kerfed light beyond
                ourselves reach for his fingers reaching for her hair

Two larval bodies naked with faces
        and seared straw in their hair hold our looking
            to the dark back of and beyond

INTERVIEW (FRAGMENTS)

Sees
    what I'm
        doing says
            No not
                that would
           look better
      like this

                            Pretty
                        good with
                  my hands I can
              do this
            (demonstrating)
        or this but
      the source is
        body-core and
          a hand held
            out (demonstrating)
              is always
                greedy-
          ness I prefer
            this (spinning
        hand inward)
      I moved
    my arm that
      way (extending it)
        until I realized
          I can move it
            instead from

                                                  here (dis-
                                          articulating her
                              shoulder)

          I ruined it
                    she says (in English)

ROAD-ENTERING

Nothing but. In care of, advanced.

With her eyelids, drawn. His

steps unchalked, the

backthrown throat. *Nothing but*

in care of thee. So dedicated

to closeness. In the singed

nothing. Against what

must ensue. Blackbrushed

with hair. Even in

dream, advanced. Ravened

with a feather. Into this

terminal tempest. What

must ensue. Who have

exchanged eyes.

NAKED

Naked and the long striations of shadow at her ribs and haunch quiver as she breathes.

Naked between exhalation and—

Naked with hidden fans blowing, a few feathers undulating on the heap.

Naked, his face upside down, forehead wrinkled, eyes sliced.

Naked and prostrate she slides her torso toward him, her arms dragging behind her.

Naked of narrative.

Naked as in unprepared for every eventuality.

Naked, and still we enter the tragedy.

Naked yet their nearness is irretrievable. Close and remote, immune to us.

Naked the abyss in those who observe in them the drama of their own grief.

So naked that sound disappears and the witnesses are overwhelmed by the intensity of two bodies passing silence between them.

Naked, her breathing more hidden than his. As her shoulder rises, a feather falls.

Naked as pupas. Ensorcelled in interiority.

Naked but not mute.

Naked peristalsis of breath. Rippling from his ribs into his pelvic girdle.

Naked as the lamps dim, days and nights passing.

Naked and listening for him, she wonders has he fallen asleep?

Naked to smells whisked-in by the audience. Softly coming going softly.

Naked where the long stretch of femur draws washlight.

Naked enough to feel cool air sucked below the hanging canvas.

Naked in a genesis before origin.

Naked in the scorched clearing with its molted feather heap.

Naked, the distance between them is the distance between each of us. Provision for our attunement.

Naked rolling toward him as he turns to meet her in the longing we share.

Naked in the first morning of an afterworld.

Naked as gels change, she ruddies, he glowers albescent.

Naked, the image whole but its absorption is insufficient.

Naked pale arm extending like a snail's horn and at the point of contact, withdrawn. Tenderness and its attendant terror.

Naked presence before which no relief.

Naked and two visitors move away to free the bench for an old couple.

Naked and when they tense, we tense reflexively, testing an empathic range of motion.

Naked and liminally aware. About to emerge. And we too at the verge of—

Naked and the small nipples pebbled on his expanding chest.

Naked and promoted to the lip of arousal.

Naked and through six hours of performance, he suppresses last night's cough.

Naked, there is no more to come. It does not arrive. There is no more to come. And it arrives.

Naked and behind them, the volcanic.

Naked and charged with immanence.

Naked the force that arches her lower back and plunges through her extensible leg.